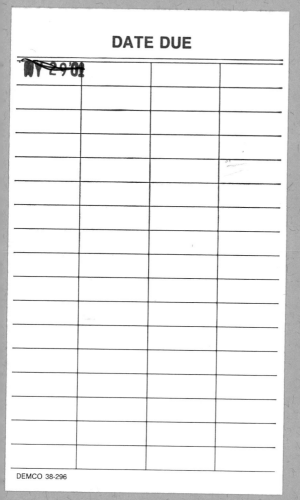

DATE DUE

MY 29'01			

DEMCO 38-296

The Torrent and
The Night Before
Edwin Arlington
Robinson

K

The Torrent and The Night Before

Edwin Arlington Robinson

A FACSIMILE EDITION
AFTER 100 YEARS
OF HIS FIRST BOOK

AFTERWORD BY
DONALD JUSTICE

TILBURY HOUSE, PUBLISHERS
GARDINER, MAINE

First Edition, May, 1996

Printing and Binding: Bookcrafters, Chelsea,
  Michigan.

The Torrent and
The Night Before

THE TORRENT
AND THE NIGHT BEFORE
BY EDWIN ARLINGTON
ROBINSON, GARDINER
MAINE, 1889-1896

Qui pourrais-je imiter pour être original ?
Coppée

PRINTED FOR THE AUTHOR
MDCCCXCVI

The Riverside Press, Cambridge, Mass., U. S. A.
Printed by H. O. Houghton and Company.

This book is dedicated to any man, woman, or critic who will cut the edges of it. — I have done the top.

THE TORRENT

I FOUND a torrent falling in a glen
Where the sun's light shone silvered and leaf-
      split ;
The boom, the foam, and the mad flash of it
All made a magic symphony ; but when
I thought upon the coming of hard men
To cut those patriarchal trees away,
And turn to gold the silver of that spray,
I shuddered.   But a gladness now and then
Did wake me to myself till I was glad
In earnest, and was welcoming the time
For screaming saws to sound above the chime
Of idle waters, and for me to know
The jealous visionings that I had had
Were steps to the great place where trees and
      torrents go.

AARON STARK

WITHAL a meagre man was Aaron Stark —
Cursed and unkempt, shrewd, shrivelled, and
      morose :
A miser was he, with a miser's nose,
And eyes like little dollars in the dark.
His thin, pinched mouth was nothing but a mark ;
And when he spoke there came like sullen blows
Through scattered fangs a few snarled words
      and close,
As if a cur were chary of its bark.

Glad for the murmur of his hard renown,
Year after year he shambled through the town,—
A loveless exile moving with a staff;
And oftentimes there crept into his ears.
A sound of alien pity, touched with tears, —
And then (and only then) did Aaron laugh.

THE DEAD VILLAGE

HERE there is death. But even here, they say —
Here where the dull sun shines this afternoon
As desolate as ever the dead moon
Did glimmer on dead Sardis — men were gay;
And there were little children here to play,
With small soft hands that once did keep in tune
The strings that stretch from heaven, till too soon
The change came, and the music passed away.

Now there is nothing but the ghosts of things:
No life, no love, no children, and no men;
And over the forgotten place there clings
The strange and unrememberable light
That is in dreams. — The music failed, and then
God frowned, and shut the village from his sight.

BALLADE OF A SHIP

DOWN by the flash of the restless water
The dim White Ship like a white bird lay;
Laughing at life and the world they sought her,
And out she swung to the silvering bay.
Then off they flew on their roystering way,
And the keen moon fired the light foam flying
Up from the flood where the faint stars play,
And the bones of the brave in the wave are lying.

'T was a king's fair son with a king's fair
  daughter,
And full three hundred beside, they say, —
Revelling on for the lone, cold slaughter
So soon to seize them and hide them for aye;

Nor ever they knew of a ghoul's eye spying
Their splendor a flickering phantom to stray
Where the bones of the brave in the wave are
    lying.

Through the mist of a drunken dream they
    brought her
(This wild white bird) for the sea-fiend's prey:
The pitiless reef in his hard clutch caught her,
And hurled her down where the dead men stay.
A torturing silence of wan dismay —
Shrieks and curses of mad souls dying —
Then down they sank to slumber and sway
Where the bones of the brave in the wave are
    lying.

Prince, do you sleep to the sound alway
Of the mournful surge and the sea-birds' cry-
    ing? —
Or does love still shudder and steel still slay,
Where the bones of the brave in the wave are lying?

DEAR FRIENDS

Dear friends, reproach me not for what I do,
Nor counsel me, nor pity me; nor say
That I am wearing half my life away
For bubble-work that only fools pursue.
And if my bubbles be too small for you,
Blow bigger then your own:—the games we
    play
To fill the frittered minutes of a day,
Good glasses are to read the spirit through.

And whoso reads may get him some shrewd skill;
And some unprofitable scorn resign,
To praise the very thing that he deplores: —
So friends (dear friends), remember, if you will,
The shame I win for singing is all mine,
The gold I miss for dreaming is all yours.

SONNET

WHEN we can all so excellently give
The measure of love's wisdom with a blow, —
Why can we not in turn receive it so,
And end this murmur for the life we live ?
And when we do so frantically strive
To win strange faith, why do we shun to know
That in love's elemental over-glow
God's wholeness gleams with light superlative ?

O brother men, if you have eyes at all,
Look at a branch, a bird, a child, a rose —
Or anything God ever made that grows —
Nor let the smallest vision of it slip
Till you can read, as on Belshazzar's wall,
The glory of eternal partnership!

HER EYES

UP from the street and the crowds that went,
Morning and midnight, to and fro,
Still was the room where his days he spent,
And the stars were bleak, and the nights were slow.

Year after year, with his dream shut fast,
He suffered and strove till his eyes were dim
For the love that his brushes had earned at last, —
And the whole world rang with the praise of him.

But he cloaked his triumph, and searched, instead,
Till his cheeks were sere and his hairs were gray, —
" There are women enough, God knows," he
        said. . . .
"There are stars enough—when the sun's away."

Then he went back to the same still room
That had held his dream in the long ago,
When he buried his days in a nameless tomb,
And the stars were bleak, and the nights were slow.

And a passionate humor seized him there —
Seized him and held him, until there grew

Like life on his canvas, — glowing and fair,
A perilous face — and an angel's, too.

Angel and maiden, and all in one.
All but the eyes. — They were there, but yet
They seemed somehow like a soul half done. —
What was the matter ? — Did God forget ? . . .

But he wrought them at last with a skill so sure
That her eyes were the eyes of a deathless
     woman, —
With a gleam of heaven to make them pure,
And a glimmer of hell to make them human.

God never forgets. — And he worships her
There in that same still room of his,
For his wife, and his constant arbiter
Of the world that was and the world that is.

And he wonders yet what her love could be
To punish him after that strife so grim ; —
But the longer he lives with her eyes to see,
The plainer it all comes back to him.

SONNET

THE master and the slave go hand in hand,
Though touch be lost. The poet is a slave,
And there be kings do sorrowfully crave
The joyance that a scullion may command.
But ah, the sonnet-slave must understand
The mission of his bondage, or the grave
May clasp his bones or ever he shall save
The perfect word that is the poet's wand.

The sonnet is a crown, whereof the rhymes
Are for Thought's purest gold the jewel-stones ;
But shapes and echoes that are never done
Will haunt the workshop, as regret sometimes
Will bring with human yearning to sad thrones
The crash of battles that are never won.

ZOLA

BECAUSE he puts the compromising chart
Of hell before your eyes, you are afraid;
Because he counts the price that you have paid
For innocence, and counts it from the start,
You loathe him. But he sees the human heart
Of God meanwhile, and in God's hand has
    weighed
Your squeamish and emasculate crusade
Against the grim dominion of his art.

Never until we conquer the uncouth
Connivings of our shamed indifference
(We call it Christian faith !) are we to scan
The racked and shrieking hideousness of Truth
To find, in hate's polluted self-defence
Throbbing, the pulse, the divine heart of man.

BALLADE

IN dreams I crossed a barren land,
A land of ruin, far away;
Around me hung on every hand
A deathful stillness of decay;
And silent, as in bleak dismay
That song should thus forsaken be,
On that forgotten ground there lay
The broken flutes of Arcady.

The forest that was all so grand
When pipes and tabors had their sway
Stood leafless now, a ghostly band
Of skeletons in cold array.
A lonely surge of ancient spray
Told of an unforgetful sea,
But iron blows had hushed for aye
The broken flutes of Arcady.

No more by summer breezes fanned,
The place was desolate and gray;

But still my dream was to command
New life into that shrunken clay.
I tried it. — Yes, you scan to-day,
With uncommiserating glee,
The songs of one who strove to play
The broken flutes of Arcady.

ENVOY

So, Rock, I join the common fray,
To fight where Mammon may decree;
And leave, to crumble as they may,
The broken flutes of Arcady.

FOR SOME POEMS
BY MATTHEW ARNOLD

SWEEPING the chords of Hellas with firm hand
He wakes lost echoes from song's classic shore,
And brings their crystal cadence back once more
To touch the clouds and sorrows of a land
Where God's truth, cramped and fettered with
    a band
Of iron creeds, he cheers with golden lore
Of heroes and the men that long before
Wrought the romance of ages yet unscanned.

Still does a cry through sad Valhalla go
For Balder, pierced with Lok's unhappy spray —
For Balder, all but spared by Frea's charms;
And still does art's imperial vista show,
On the hushed sands of Oxus, far away,
Young Sohrab dying in his father's arms.

GEORGE CRABBE

GIVE him the darkest inch your shelf allows,
Hide him in lonely garrets, if you will, —
But his hard, human pulse is throbbing still
With the sure strength that fearless truth en-
    dows: —

In spite of all fine science disavows,
Of his plain excellence and stubborn skill
There yet remains what fashion cannot kill,
Though years have thinned the laurel from his
    brows.

Whether or not we read him, we can feel
From time to time the vigor of his name
Against us like a finger for the shame
And emptiness of what our souls reveal
In books that are as altars where we kneel
To consecrate the flicker, not the flame.

SONNET

OH, for a poet — for a beacon bright
To rift this changeless glimmer of dead gray:
To spirit back the Muses, long astray,
And flush Parnassus with a newer light:
To put these little sonnet-men to flight
Who fashion, in a shrewd mechanic way,
Songs without souls that flicker for a day
To vanish in irrevocable night.

What does it mean, this barren age of ours?
Here are the men, the women, and the flowers, —
The seasons, and the sunset, as before.
What does it mean? — Shall not one bard arise
To wrench one banner from the western skies,
And mark it with his name for evermore?

THE ALTAR

ALONE, remote, nor witting where I went,
I found an altar builded in a dream —
A fiery place, whereof there was a gleam
So swift, so searching, and so eloquent
Of upward promise that love's murmur, blent
With sorrow's warning, gave but a supreme
Unending impulse to that human stream
Whose flood was all for the flame's fury bent.

Alas! I said, — the world is in the wrong. —
But the same quenchless fever of unrest
That thrilled the foremost of that martyred throng
Thrilled me, and I awoke . . . and was the same
Bewildered insect plunging for the flame
That burns, and must burn somehow for the best.

THE HOUSE ON THE HILL

THEY are all gone away,
The House is shut and still,
There is nothing more to say.

Through broken walls and gray
The winds blow bleak and shrill;
They are all gone away.

Nor is there one to-day
To speak them good or ill:
There is nothing more to say.

Why is it then we stray
Around that sunken sill?
They are all gone away,

And our poor fancy-play
For them is wasted skill:
There is nothing more to say.

There is ruin and decay
In the House on the Hill:
They are all gone away,
There is nothing more to say.

THE WILDERNESS

COME away! come away! — there's a frost along
    the marshes,
And a frozen wind that skims the shoal where
    it shakes the dead black water;
There's a moan across the lowland and a wail-
    ing through the woodland

Of a dirge that sings to send us back to the arms
    of those that love us.
There is nothing left but ashes now where the
    crimson chills of autumn
Put off the summer's languor with a touch that
    made us glad
For the glory that is gone from us, with a flight
    we cannot follow,
To the slopes of other valleys and the sounds of
    other shores.

Come away! come away! — you can hear them
    calling, calling,
Calling us to come to them, and roam no more.
Over there beyond the ridges and the land that lies
    between us,
There's an old song calling us to come!

Come away! come away! — for the scenes we
    leave behind us
Are barren for the lights of home and a flame
    that's young forever;
And the lonely trees around us creak the warn-
    ing of the night-wind,
That love and all the dreams of love are away
    beyond the mountains.
The songs that call for us to-night, they have
    called for men before us, —
And the winds that blow the message, they have
    blown ten thousand years;
But this will end our wander-time, for we know
    the joy that waits us
In the strangeness of home-coming, and a faith-
    ful woman's eyes.

Come away! come away! — there is nothing now
    to cheer us —
Nothing now to comfort us, but love's road home:
Over there beyond the darkness there's a window
    gleams to greet us,
And a warm hearth waits for us within.

Come away! come away! — or the roving-fiend
  will hold us,
And make us all to dwell with him to the end
  of human faring:
There are no men yet can leave him when his
  hands are clutched upon them,
There are none will own his enmity, there are
  none will call him brother. —
So we'll be up and on the way, and the less we
  brag the better
For the freedom that God gave us and the dread
  we do not know: —
The frost that skips the willow-leaf will again
  be back to blight it,
And the doom we cannot fly from is the doom
  we do not see.

Come away! come away! there are dead men all
  around us —
Frozen men that mock us with a wild, hard laugh
That shrieks and sinks and whimpers in the shrill
  November rushes,
And the long fall wind on the lake.

LUKE HAVERGAL

Go to the western gate, Luke Havergal, —
There where the vines cling crimson on the
  wall, —
And in the twilight wait for what will come.
The wind will moan, the leaves will whisper
  some —
Whisper of her, and strike you as they fall;
But go, and if you trust her she will call, —
Go to the western gate, Luke Havergal, —
Luke Havergal.

No, there is not a dawn in eastern skies
To rift the fiery night that's in your eyes ;
But there, where western glooms are gathering,
The dark will end the dark, if anything: —

God slays Himself with every leaf that flies,
And hell is more than half of paradise. —
No, there is not a dawn in eastern skies,
In eastern skies.

Out of a grave I come to tell you this, —
Out of a grave I come to quench the kiss
That flames upon your forehead with a glow
That blinds you to the way that you must go.
Yes, there is yet one way to where she is —
Bitter, but one that faith can never miss. —
Out of a grave I come to tell you this,
To tell you this.

There is the western gate, Luke Havergal,
There are the crimson leaves upon the wall.
Go, — for the winds are tearing them away —
Nor think to riddle the dead words they say,
Nor any more to feel them as they fall;
But go! and if you trust her she will call. —
There is the western gate, Luke Havergal, —
Luke Havergal.

THE CHORUS OF OLD MEN IN "ÆGEUS"

YE gods that have a home beyond the world,
Ye that have eyes for all man's agony,
Ye that have seen this woe that we have seen, —
Look with a just regard,
And with an even grace,
Here on the shattered corpse of a shattered king,
Here on a suffering world where men grow old
And wander like sad shadows till, at last,
Out of the flare of life,
Out of the whirl of years,
Into the mist they go,
Into the mist of death.

O shades of you that loved him long before
The cruel threads of that black sail were spun,

May loyal arms and ancient welcomings
Receive him once again
Who now no longer moves
Here in this flickering dance of changing days
Where a battle is lost and won for a withered
    wreath,
And the black master Death is over all,
To chill with his approach,
To level with his touch,
The reigning strength of youth,
The fluttered heart of age.

Woe for the fateful day when Delphi's word
    was lost —
Woe for the loveless prince of Æthra's line!
Woe for a father's tears and the curse of a
    king's release —
Woe for the wings of pride and the shafts of
    doom! —
And thou the saddest wind
That ever blew from Crete,
Sing the fell tidings back to that thrice un-
    happy ship! —
Sing to the western flame,
Sing to the dying foam,
A dirge for the sundered years and a dirge for
    the years to be!

Better his end had been as the end of a cloud-
    less day,
Bright, by the word of Zeus, with a golden star,
Wrought of a golden fame, and flung to the
    central sky,
To gleam on a stormless tomb for evermore: —
Whether or not there fell
To the touch of an alien hand
The sheen of his purple robe and the shine of
    his diadem,
Better his end had been
To die as an old man dies, —
But the fates are ever the fates, and a crown is
    ever a crown.

THE MIRACLE

" DEAR brother, dearest friend, when I am dead,
And you shall see no more this face of mine,
Let nothing but red roses be the sign
Of the white life I lost for him," she said;
" No, do not curse him, — pity him instead;
Forgive him! — forgive me! . . . God's anodyne
For human hate is pity; and the wine
That makes men wise, forgiveness. I have read
Love's message in love's murder, and I die."
And so they laid her just where she would lie, —
Under red roses. Red they bloomed and fell;
But when flushed autumn and the snows went by,
And spring came, — lo, from every bud's green
    shell
Burst a white blossom. — Can love reason why?

HORACE TO LEUCONOE

I PRAY you not, Leuconoe, to pore
With unpermitted eyes on what may be
Appointed by the gods for you and me,
Nor on Chaldean figures any more.
'T were infinitely better to implore
The present only: — whether Jove decree
More winters yet to come, or whether he
Make even this, whose hard, wave-eaten shore
Shatters the Tuscan seas to-day, the last —
Be wise withal, and rack your wine, nor fill
Your bosom with large hopes; for while I sing,
The envious close of time is narrowing: —
So seize the day, — or ever it be past —
And let the morrow come for what it will.

THE BALLADE
OF DEAD FRIENDS

As we the withered ferns
By the roadway lying,
Time, the jester, spurns

All our prayers and prying, —
All our tears and sighing,
Sorrow, change, and woe, —
All our where-and-whying
For friends that come and go.

Life awakes and burns,
Age and death defying,
Till at last it learns
All but Love is dying; —
Love 's the trade we 're plying,
God has willed it so;
Shrouds are what we 're buying
For friends that come and go.

Man forever yearns
For the thing that 's flying:
Everywhere he turns,
Men to dust are drying —
Dust that wanders, eyeing
(With eyes that hardly glow)
New faces, dimly spying
For friends that come and go.

ENVOY

And thus we all are nighing
The truth we fear to know:
Death will end our crying
For friends that come and go.

VILLANELLE OF CHANGE

SINCE Persia fell at Marathon,
The yellow years have gathered fast:
Long centuries have come and gone.

And yet (they say) the place will don
A phantom fury of the past,
Since Persia fell at Marathon;

And as of old, when Helicon
Trembled and swayed with rapture vast
(Long centuries have come and gone),

This ancient plain, when night comes on,
Shakes to a ghostly battle-blast,
Since Persia fell at Marathon. —

But into soundless Acheron
The glory of Greek shame was cast:
Long centuries have come and gone,

The suns of Hellas have all shone,
The first has fallen to the last: —
Since Persia fell at Marathon,
Long centuries have come and gone.

THOMAS HOOD

THE man who cloaked his bitterness within
This winding-sheet of puns and pleasantries,
God never gave to look with common eyes
Upon a world of anguish and of sin: —
His brother was the branded man of Lynn;
And there are woven with his jollities
The nameless and eternal tragedies
That render hope and hopelessness akin.

We laugh, and crown him; but anon we feel
A still chord sorrow swept, — a weird unrest;
And thin dim shadows home to midnight steal,
As if the very ghost of mirth were dead —
As if the joys of time to dreams had fled,
Or sailed away with Ines to the West.

FOR A BOOK
BY THOMAS HARDY

WITH searching feet, through dark circuitous
    ways,
I plunged and stumbled; round me, far and near,

Quaint hordes of eyeless phantoms did appear,
Twisting and turning in a bootless chase, —
When, like an exile given by God's grace
To feel once more a human atmosphere,
I caught the world's first murmur, large and
    clear,
Flung from a singing river's endless race.

Then, through a magic twilight from below,
I heard its grand sad song as in a dream:
Life's wild infinity of mirth and woe
It sang me; and, with many a changing gleam,
Across the music of its onward flow,
I saw the cottage lights of Wessex beam.

SUPREMACY

THERE is a drear and lonely tract of hell
From all the common gloom removed afar:
A flat, sad land it is, where shadows are
Whose lorn estate my verse may never tell.
I walked among them and I knew them well:
Men I had slandered on life's little star
For churls and sluggards; and I knew the scar
Upon their brows of woe ineffable.

But as I went majestic on my way,
Into the dark they vanished, one by one,
Till, with a shaft of God's eternal day,
The dream of all my glory was undone, —
And, with a fool's importunate dismay,
I heard the dead men singing in the sun.

THREE QUATRAINS

I

As long as Fame's imperious music rings
Will poets mock it with crowned words august;
And haggard men will clamber to be kings
As long as Glory weighs itself in dust.

II

Drink to the splendor of the unfulfilled,
Nor shudder for the revels that are done: —
The wines that flushed Lucullus are all spilled,
The strings that Nero fingered are all gone.

III

We cannot crown ourselves with everything,
Nor can we coax the Fates for us to quarrel: —
No matter what we are, or what we sing,
Time finds a withered leaf in every laurel.

FOR CALDERON

AND now, my brother, it is time
For me to tell the truth to you:
To tell the story of a crime
As black as Mona's eyes were blue. —
Yes, here to-night, before I die,
I 'll speak the words that burn in me;
And you may send them, bye-and-bye,
To Calderon across the sea.

Now get some paper and a pen,
And sit right here, beside my bed.
Write every word I say, and then —
And then . . . well, what then? — I 'll be
    dead! —
. . . But here I am alive enough,
And I remember all I 've done . . .
God knows what I was thinking of! —
But send it home — to Calderon.

And you, Francisco, brother, say, —
What is there for a man like me? —
I tell you God sounds far away —
As far — almost as far — as she!
I killed her! . . . Yes, I poisoned her —
So slowly that she never knew . . .
Francisco, — I 'm a murderer. —
Now tell me what there is to do!

To die — of course ; but after that,
I wonder if I live again!
And if I live again, for what? —
To suffer ? . . . Bah! — there is no pain
But one; and that I know so well
That I can shame the devil's eyes! . . .
For twenty years I 've heard in hell
What Mona sings in Paradise!

Strange, that a little Northern girl
Should love my brother Calderon,
And set my brain so in a whirl
That I was mad till she was gone! . . .
I wonder if all men be such
As I ? — I wonder what love is! —
I never loved her very much
Until I saw that she was his; —

And then I knew that I was lost:
And then — I knew that I was mad. —
I reasoned what it all would cost,
But that was nothing. — I was glad
To feel myself so foul a thing! —
And I was glad for Calderon. . . .
My God! if he could hear her sing
Just once, as I do! — There! she 's done. . . .

No, it was only something wrong
A minute — something in my head. —
God, no ! — she 'll never stop that song
As long as I 'm alive or dead!
As long as I am here or there,
She 'll sing to me, a murderer! —
Well, I suppose the gods are fair. . . .
I killed her . . . yes, I poisoned her!

But you, Francisco, — you are young; —
So take my hand and hear me, now: —
There are no lies upon your tongue,
There is no guilt upon your brow. —
But there is blood upon your name ? —
And blood, you say, will rust the steel

That strikes for honor or for shame? . . .
Francisco, it is fear you feel! —

And such a miserable fear
That you, my boy, will call it pride; —
But you will grope from year to year
Until at last the clouds divide,
And all at once you meet the truth,
And curse yourself, with helpless rage,
For something you have lost with youth
And found again, too late, with age.

The truth, my brother, is just this: —
Your title here is nothing more
Or less than what your courage is:
The man must put himself before
The name, and once the master stay
Forever — or forever fall. —
Good-bye! — Remember what I say . . .
Good-bye! — Good-bye! . . . And that was all.

The lips were still: the man was dead. —
Francisco, with a weird surprise,
Stood like a stranger by the bed,
And there were no tears in his eyes.
But in his heart there was a grief
Too strong for human tears to free, —
And in his hand a written leaf
For Calderon across the sea.

JOHN EVERELDOWN

WHERE are you going to-night, to-night, —
Where are you going, John Evereldown?
There's never the sign of a star in sight,
Nor a lamp that's nearer than Tilbury Town.
Why do you stare as a dead man might?
Where are you pointing away from the light?
And where are you going to-night, to-night, —
Where are you going, John Evereldown?

Right through the forest, where none can see,
There's where I'm going to Tilbury Town.
The men are asleep — or awake, may be —
But the women are calling John Evereldown.
Ever and ever they call for me,
And while they call can a man be free? —
So right through the forest, where none can
    see,
There's where I'm going to Tilbury Town.

But why are you going so late, so late, —
Why are you going, John Evereldown?
Though the road be smooth and the path be
    straight,
There are two long leagues to Tilbury Town.
Come in by the fire, old man, and wait!
Why do you chatter out there by the gate?
And why are you going so late, so late, —
Why are you going, John Evereldown?

I follow the women wherever they call, —
That's why I'm going to Tilbury Town.
God knows if I pray to be done with it all,
But God is no friend to John Evereldown. —
So the clouds may come and the rain may fall,
The shadows may creep and the dead men
    crawl; —
But I follow the women wherever they call,
And that's why I'm going to Tilbury Town.

THE WORLD

SOME are the brothers of all humankind,
And own them, whatsoever their estate;
And some, for sorrow and self-scorn, are blind
With enmity for man's unguarded fate.

For some there is a music all day long
Like flutes in paradise, they are so glad;
And there is hell's eternal under-song
Of curses and the cries of men gone mad.

Some say the Scheme with love stands luminous,
Some say 't were better back to chaos hurled;
And so 't is what we are that makes for us
The measure and the meaning of the world.

CREDO

I CANNOT find my way : there is no star
In all the shrouded heavens anywhere;
And there is not a whisper in the air
Of any living voice but one so far
That I can hear it only as a bar
Of lost, imperial music, played when fair
And angel fingers wove, and unaware,
Dead leaves to garlands where no roses are.

No, there is not a glimmer, nor a call,
For one that welcomes, welcomes when he fears,
The black and awful chaos of the night: —
For through it all — above, beyond it all —
I know the far-sent message of the years,
I feel the coming glory of the Light!

THE CHILDREN OF THE NIGHT

FOR those that never know the light,
The darkness is a sullen thing;
And they, the Children of the Night,
Seem lost in Fortune's winnowing.

But some are strong and some are weak, —
And there's the story.   House and home
Are shut from countless hearts that seek
World-refuge that will never come.

And if there be no other life,
And if there be no other chance
To weigh their sorrow and their strife
Than in the scales of circumstance —

'T were better, ere the sun go down
Upon the first day we embark,

In life's embittered sea to drown
Than sail forever in the dark.

But if there be a soul on earth
So blinded with its own misuse
Of man's revealed, incessant worth,
Or worn with anguish that it views

No light but for a mortal eye —
No rest but of a mortal sleep —
No God but in a prophet's lie —
No faith for " honest doubt " to keep —

If there be nothing, good or bad,
But chaos for a soul to trust, —
God counts it for a soul gone mad,
And if God be God, He is just.

And if God be God, He is Love; —
And though the Dawn be still so dim,
It shows us we have played enough
With creeds that make a fiend of Him.

There is one creed, and only one,
That glorifies God's excellence; —
So cherish, that His will be done,
The common creed of common sense.

It is the crimson, not the gray,
That charms the twilight of all time;
It is the promise of the day
That makes the starry sky sublime ;

It is the faith within the fear
That holds us to the life we curse; —
So let us in ourselves revere
The Self which is the Universe!

Let us, the Children of the Night,
Put off the cloak that hides the scar! —
Let us be Children of the Light,
And tell the ages what we are!

THE CLERKS

I DID not think that I should find them there
When I came back again ; but there they stood,
As in the days they dreamed of when young
    blood
Was in their cheeks and women called them
    fair.
Be sure, they met me with an ancient air, —
And yes, there was a shop-worn brotherhood
About them ; but the men were just as good,
And just as human as they ever were.

And you that ache so much to be sublime,
And you that feed yourselves with your de-
    scent,
What comes of all your visions and your
    fears? —
Poets and kings are but the clerks of Time,
Tiering the same dull webs of discontent,
Clipping the same sad alnage of the years.

A BALLADE BY THE FIRE

SLOWLY I smoke and hug my knee,
The while a witless masquerade
Of things that only children see
Floats in a mist of light and shade :
They pass, a flimsy cavalcade,
And with a weak, remindful glow,
The falling embers break and fade,
As one by one the phantoms go.

Then, with a melancholy glee
To think where once my fancy strayed,
I muse on what the years may be
Whose coming tales are all unsaid,
Till tongs and shovel, snugly laid
Within their shadowed niches, grow
By grim degrees to pick and spade,
As one by one the phantoms go.

But then, what though the mystic Three
Around me ply their merry trade? —
And Charon soon may carry me
Across the gloomy Stygian glade? —
Be up, my soul! nor be afraid
Of what some unborn year may show; —
But mind your human debts are paid,
As one by one the phantoms go.

Life is the game that must be played:
This truth at least, good friend, we know. —
So live and laugh, nor be dismayed
As one by one the phantoms go.

ON THE NIGHT OF
A FRIEND'S WEDDING

IF ever I am old, and all alone,
I shall have killed one grief, at any rate;
For then, thank God, I shall not have to wait
Much longer for the sheaves that I have sown.
The devil only knows what I have done,
But here I am, and here are six or eight
Good friends who most ingenuously prate
About my songs to such and such a one.

But everything is all askew to-night, —
As if the time were come, or almost come,
For their untenanted mirage of me
To lose itself and crumble out of sight —
Like a tall ship that floats above the foam
A little while, and then breaks utterly.

VERLAINE

WHY do you dig like long-clawed scavengers
To touch the covered corpse of him that fled
The uplands for the fens and rioted
Like a sick satyr with doom's worshippers? —
Come! — let the grass grow there; and leave his
      verse

To tell the story of the life he led.
Let the man go: let the dead flesh be dead,
And let the worms be its biographers.

Song sloughs away the sin to find redress
In art's complete remembrance: nothing clings
For long but laurel to the stricken brow
That felt the Muse's finger; nothing less
Than hell's fulfilment of the end of things
Can blot the star that shines on Paris now.

THE GARDEN

THERE is a fenceless garden overgrown
With buds and blossoms and all sorts of leaves;
And once, among the roses and the sheaves,
The Gardener and I were there alone.
He led me to the plot where I had thrown
The fennel of my days on wasted ground,
And in that riot of sad weeds I found
The fruitage of a life that was my own.

My life! . . . Ah yes, there was my life, indeed!
And there were all the lives of humankind;
And they were like a book that I could read,
Whose every leaf, miraculously signed,
Outrolled itself from Thought's eternal seed,
Love-rooted in God's garden of the mind.

TWO SONNETS

I

JUST as I wonder at the twofold screen
Of twisted innocence that you would plait
For eyes that uncourageously await
The coming of a kingdom that has been,
So do I wonder what God's love can mean
To you that all so strangely estimate
The purpose and the consequent estate
Of one short shuddering step to the Unseen.

No, I have not your backward faith to shrink
Lone-faring from the doorway of God's home,
To find Him in the names of buried men;
Nor your ingenious recreance to think
We cherish, in the life that is to come,
The scattered features of dead friends again.

II

NEVER until our souls are strong enough
To plunge into the crater of the Scheme —
Triumphant in the flash there to redeem
Love's handsel and for evermore to slough,
Like cerements at a played-out masque, the
  rough
And reptile skins of us whereon we set
The stigma of scared years — are we to get
Where atoms and the ages are one stuff.

Nor ever shall we know the cursed waste
Of life in the beneficence divine
Of starlight and of sunlight and soul-shine
That we have squandered in sin's frail distress,
Till we have drunk, and trembled at the taste,
The mead of Thought's prophetic endlessness.

WALT WHITMAN

THE master-songs are ended, and the man
That sang them is a name.   And so is God
A name; and so is love, and life, and death,
And everything. — But we, who are too blind
To read what we have written, or what faith
Has written for us, do not understand:
We only blink, and wonder.

Last night it was the song that was the man,
But now it is the man that is the song.
We do not hear him very much to-day; —
His piercing and eternal cadence rings
Too pure for us — too powerfully pure,

Too lovingly triumphant, and too large;
But there are some that hear him, and they know
That he shall sing to-morrow for all men,
And that all time shall listen.

The master-songs are ended? — Rather say
No songs are ended that are ever sung,
And that no names are dead names.   When we
  write
Men's letters on proud marble or on sand,
We write them there forever.

KOSMOS

AH, shuddering men that falter and shrink so
To look on death, — what were the days we live,
Where life is half a struggle to forgive,
But for the love that finds us when we go?
Is God a jester? — Does he laugh and throw
Poor branded wretches here to sweat and strive
For some vague end that never shall arrive? —
And is He not yet weary of the show?

Think of it, all ye millions that have planned,
And only planned, the largess of hard youth!
Think of it, all ye builders on the sand,
Whose works are down! — Is love so small, for-
  sooth?
Be brave! — To-morrow you will understand
The doubt, the pain, the triumph, and the Truth!

AN OLD STORY

STRANGE that I did not know him then,
That friend of mine! —
I did not even show him then
One friendly sign;

But cursed him for the ways he had
To make me see
My envy of the praise he had
For praising me.

I would have rid the earth of him
Once, in my pride! . . .
I never knew the worth of him
Until he died.

A POEM FOR
MAX NORDAU

DUN shades quiver down the lone long fallow,
And thescared night shudders at the brown owl's
    cry;
The bleak reeds rattle as the winds whirl by,
And frayed leaves flutter through the clumped
    shrubs callow.

Chill dews clinging on the low cold mallow
Make a steel-keen shimmer where the spent
    stems lie;
Dun shades quiver down the lone long fallow,
And the scared night shudders at the brown
    owl's cry.

Pale stars peering through the clouds' curled
    shallow
Make a thin still flicker in a foul round sky;
Black damp shadows through the hushed air fly;
The lewd gloom wakens to a moon-sad sallow,
Dun shades quiver down the lone long fallow.

BOSTON

MY northern pines are good enough for me,
But there's a town my memory uprears —
A town that always like a friend appears,
And always in the sunrise by the sea.
And over it, somehow, there seems to be
A downward flash of something new and fierce
That ever strives to clear, but never clears
The dimness of a charmed antiquity.

I know my Boston is a counterfeit, —
A frameless imitation, all bereft

Of living nearness, noise, and common speech;
But I am glad for every glimpse of it, —
And there it is — plain as a name that's left
In letters by warm hands I cannot reach.

THE NIGHT BEFORE

" As if God made him and then wondered why."

Look you, Domine; look you, and listen.
Look in my face, first: search every line there;
Mark every feature, — chin, lip, and forehead.
Look in my eyes, and tell me the lesson
You read there; — measure my nose, and tell me
Where I am wanting. A man's nose, Domine,
Is often the cast of his inward spirit; —
So mark mine well. . . . But why do you smile
    so? —
Pity, or what? — Is it written all over,
This face of mine, with a brute's confession? —
Nothing but sin there ? nothing but hell-
    scars? —
Or is it because there is something better —
A glimmer of good, maybe, — or a shadow
Of something that's followed me down from
    childhood —
Followed me all these years and kept me,
Spite of my slips and sins and follies —
Spite of my last red sin, my murder, —
Just out of hell? — Yes? — something of that
    kind?
And you smile for that? . . . You're a good
    man, Domine! —
The one good man in the world who knows me —
My one good friend in a world that mocks me,
Here in this hard stone cage. . . . But I leave
    it
To-morrow. . . . To-morrow! — My God! am
    I crying? —
Are these things tears? — Tears! — What! am
    I frightened ? —
I who swore I should go to the scaffold

With big strong steps, and . . . No more, —
    I thank you,
But no. . . . I am all right now! . . . No! —
    listen!

I am here to be hanged: to be hanged to-mor-
    row —
At six o'clock, when the sun is rising. —
And why am I here? — Not a soul can tell you
But this poor shivering thing before you —
This fluttering wreck of the man God made
    him,
For God knows what wild reason. — Hear me,
And learn from my lips the truth of my story. —
There's nothing strange in what I shall tell
    you —
Nothing mysterious, nothing unearthly, —
But damnably human; — and you shall hear it.
Not one of those little black lawyers were told
    it;
The judge, with his big bald head, never knew
    it ;
And the jury (God rest their poor souls!) never
    dreamed it, —
Once there were three in the world who could
    tell it, —
Now there are two. There'll be two to-mor-
    row: —
You, my friend, and . . . But there's the story.

When I was a boy the world was heaven.
I never knew then that the men and the women
Who petted and called me a brave big fellow
Were ever less happy than I; but wisdom —
Which comes with the years, you know, — soon
    showed me
The secret of all my glittering childhood —
The broken key to the fairies' castle
That held my life in the fresh glad season
When I was the king of the earth. — Then
    slowly —

And yet so swiftly! — there came the know-
  ledge
That the marvelous life I had lived was my
  life;
That the glorious world I had loved was my
  world; —
And that every man and every woman
And every child was a different being,
Wrought with a different heat and fired
With passions born of a single spirit; —
That the pleasure I felt was not their pleasure,
Nor my sorrow — a kind of nameless pity
For something, I knew not what — their sorrow.
And thus was I taught my first hard lesson, —
The lesson we suffer the most in learning:
That a happy man is a man forgetful
Of all the torturing ills around him.

When or where I first met the woman
I cherished and made my wife, no matter.
Enough to say that I found her and kept her
Here in my heart with as pure a devotion
As ever Christ felt for his brothers. Forgive me
For naming his name in your patient presence;
But I feel my words, and the truth I utter
Is God's own truth. I loved that woman! —
Not for her face, but for something fairer —
Something diviner — I thought — than beauty:
I loved the spirit — the human something
That seemed to chime with my own condition,
And make soul-music when we were together;—
And we were never apart from the moment
My eyes flashed into her eyes the message
That swept itself in a quivering answer
Back through my strange lost being. My pulses
Leapt with an aching speed; and the measure
Of this great world grew small and smaller,
Till it seemed the sky and the land and the
  ocean
Closed at last in a mist all golden
Around us two. — And we stood for a season

Like gods outflung from chaos, dreaming
That we were the king and the queen of the fire
That reddened the clouds of love that held us
Blind to the new world soon to be ours —
Ours to seize and sway.   The passion
Of that great love was a nameless passion —
Bright as the blaze of the sun at noonday,
Wild as the flames of hell; but, mark you,
Never a whit less pure for its fervor.
The baseness in me (for I was human)
Burned like a worm, and perished; and nothing
Was left me then but a soul that mingled
Itself with hers, and swayed and shuddered
In fearful triumph. — When I consider
That helpless love and the cursed folly
That wrecked my life for the sake of a woman,
Who broke with a laugh the chains of her
          marriage
(Whatever the word may mean) I wonder
If all the woe was her sin, or whether
The chains themselves were enough to lead her
In love's despite to break them. . . . Sinners
And saints — I say — are rocked in the cradle,
But never are known till the will within them
Speaks in its own good time, — So I foster
Even to-night for the woman who wronged me
Nothing of hate, nor of love, but a feeling
Of still regret. — For the man . . . But hear me,
And judge for yourself: —

                          For a time the seasons
Changed and passed in a sweet succession
That seemed to me like an endless music:
Life was a rolling psalm, and the choirs
Of God were glad for our love. — I fancied
All this, and more than I dare to tell you
To-night, — yes, more than I dare to remem-
          ber; —
And then . . . . well, the music stopped. There
          are moments
In all men's lives when it stops, I fancy, —

Or seems to stop, — till it comes to cheer them
Again with a larger sound.   The curtain
Of life just then is lifted a little
To give to their sight new joys — new sorrows —
Or nothing at all, sometimes. — I was watching
The slow sweet scenes of a golden picture,
Flushed and alive with a long delusion
That made the murmur of home, when I shud-
        dered
And felt like a knife that awful silence
That comes when the music goes — forever.
The truth came over my life like a darkness
Over a forest where one man wanders,
Worse than alone.   For a time I staggered
And stumbled on with a weak persistence
After the phantom of hope that darted
And dodged like a frightened thing before me,
To quit me at last, and vanish.   Nothing
Was left me then but the curse of living
And bearing through all my days the fever
And thirst of a poisoned love. — Were I stronger,
Or weaker, perhaps my scorn had saved me —
Given me strength to crush my sorrow
With hate for her and the world that praised
        her —
To have left her, then and there, — to have con-
        quered
That old false life with a new and a wiser; —
Such things are easy in words. . . . You listen,
And frown, I suppose, that I never mention
That beautiful word, *forgive !* — I forgave her
First of all; and I praised kind heaven
That I was a brave clean man to do it;
And then I tried to forget. — Forgiveness! . . .
What does it mean when the one forgiven
Shivers and weeps and clings and kisses
The credulous fool that holds her, and tells
        him
A thousand things of a good man's mercy,
And then slips off with a laugh and plunges
Back to the sin she has quit for a season

To tell him that hell and the world are better
For her than a prophet's heaven? — Believe me,
The love that dies ere its flames are wasted
In search of an alien soul is better,
Better by far than the lonely passion
That burns back into the heart that feeds it.
For I loved her still; and the more she mocked
    me, —
Fooled with her endless pleading promise
Of future faith, the more I believed her
The penitent thing she seemed; and the stronger
Her choking arms and her small hot kisses
Bound me and burned my brain to pity,
The more she grew to the heavenly creature
That brightened the life I had lost forever.
The truth was gone somehow for the moment;
The curtain fell for a time; and I fancied
We were again like gods together,
Loving again with the old glad rapture. —
But the scenes like these, too often repeated,
Failed at last and her guile was wasted,
I made an end of her shrewd caresses
And told her a few straight words. She took
    them
Full at their worth — and the farce was over.

At first my dreams of the past upheld me,
But they were a short support: the present
Pushed them away, and I fell. The mission
Of life (whatever it was) was blasted;
My game was lost. And I met the winner
Of that foul deal as a sick slave gathers
His painful strength at the sight of his master;
And when he was past I cursed him, fearful
Of that strange chance which makes us mighty
Or mean, or both. — I cursed him and hated
The stones he pressed with his heel; I followed
His easy march with a backward envy,
And cursed myself for the beast within me. —
But pride is the master of love; and the vision
Of those old days grew faint and fainter: —

The counterfeit wife my mercy sheltered
Was nothing now but a woman; — a woman
Out of my way, and out of my nature. —
My battle with blinded love was over,
My battle with aching pride beginning. —
If I was the loser at first, I wonder
If I am the winner now! . . . I doubt it.
My life is a losing game; and to-morrow . . .
To-morrow! . . . Christ! — did I say to-
  morrow ? . . .
Is your brandy good for death?. . . There; —
  listen: —

When love goes out, and a man is driven
To shun mankind for the scars that make him
A joke for all chattering tongues, he carries
A double burden. The woes I suffered
After that hard betrayal made me
Pity, at first, all breathing creatures
On this bewildered earth. I studied
Their faces and made for myself the story
Of all their scattered lives. Like brothers
And sisters they seemed to me then; and I
  nourished
A stranger friendship wrought in my fancy
Between those people and me. — But somehow,
As time went on, there came queer glances
Out of their eyes; and the shame that stung me
Harassed my pride with a crazed impression
That every face in the surging city
Was turned to me; and I saw sly whispers,
Now and then, as I walked and wearied
My wasted life twice over in bearing
With all my sorrow the sorrows of others, —
Till I found myself their fool. Then I trem-
  bled —
A poor scared thing — and their prying faces
Told me the ghastly truth: — they were laughing
At me, and my fate. My God, I could feel it —
That laughter! — And then the children caught
  it;

And I, like a struck dog, crept and listened.
And then when I met the man who had weakened
A woman's love to his own desire,
It seemed to me that all hell were laughing
In fiendish concert! — I was their victim —
And his, and hate's.   And there was the strug-
    gle ! —
As long as the earth we tread holds something
A tortured heart can love, the meaning
Of life is not wholly blurred; but after
The last loved thing in the world has left us,
We know the triumph of hate.   The glory
Of good goes out forever; the beacon
Of sin is the light that leads us downward —
Down to the fiery end.   The road runs
Right through hell; and the souls that follow
The cursed ways where its windings lead them
Suffer enough, I say, to merit
All grace that a God can give. — The fashion
Of our belief is to lift all beings
Born for a life that knows no struggle
In sin's tight snares to eternal glory —
All apart from the branded millions
Who carry through life their faces graven
With sure brute scars that tell the story
Of their foul, fated passions. — Science
Has yet no salve to smooth or soften
The cradle-scars of a tyrant's visage; —
No drug to purge from the vital essence
Of souls the sleeping venom.   Virtue
May flower in hell, when its roots are twisted
And wound with the roots of vice; but the stronger
Never is known till there comes that battle
With sin to prove the victor.   Perilous
Things are these demons we call our passions—
Slaves are we of their roving fancies,
Fools of their devilish glee. — You think me,
I know, in this maundering way designing
To lighten the load of my guilt and cast it
Half on the shoulders of God . . . But hear
    me ! —

I 'm partly a man — for all my weakness, —
If weakness it were to stand and murder
Before men's eyes the man who had murdered
Me, and driven my burning forehead
With horns for the world to laugh at . . . Trust
    me ! —
And try to believe my words but a portion
Of what God's purpose made me ! — The coward
Within me cries for this; — and I beg you
Now, as I come to the end, to remember
That women and men are on earth to travel
All on a different road. Hereafter
The roads may meet . . . I trust in something —
I know not what . . .

                Well, this was the way of it: —
Stung with the shame and the secret fury
That comes to the man who has thrown his pittance
Of self at a traitor's feet, I wandered
Weeks and weeks in a baffled frenzy,
Till at last the devil spoke. I heard him,
And laughed at the love that strove to touch
    me —
The dead, lost love; — and I gripped the demon
Close to my breast, and held him, praising
The fates and the furies that gave me the courage
To follow his wild command. — Forgetful
Of all to come when the work was over —
There came to me then no stony vision
Of these three hundred days — I cherished
An awful joy in my brain. I pondered
And weighed the thing in my mind, and gloried
In life to think that I was to conquer
Death at his own dark door, — and chuckled
To think of it done so cleanly. — One evening
I knew that my time had come. I shuddered
A little, but rather for doubt than terror,
And followed him — led by the nameless devil
I worshipped and called my brother. — The city
Shone like a dream that night: the windows
Flashed with a piercing flame, and the pavements

Pulsed and swayed with a warmth — or some-
    thing
That seemed so then to my feet — and thrilled
    me
With a quick, dizzy joy; and the women
And men, like marvellous things of magic,
Floated and laughed and sang by my shoulder,
Sent with a wizard motion. Through it
And over and under it all there sounded
A murmur of life, like bees; and I listened
And laughed again to think of the flower
That grew, blood red, for me! . . . This fellow
Was one of the popular sort who flourish
Uuruffled'where gods would fall. For a conscience
He carried a snug deceit that made him
The man of the time and the place, whatever
The time or the place might be: — were he
    sounding
With a genial craft that cloaked its purpose,
Nigh to itself, the depth of a woman
Fooled with his brainless art, — or sending
The midnight home with songs and bottles, —
The cad was there, and his ease forever
Shone with the smooth and slippery polish
That tells the snake. — That night he drifted
Into an up-town haunt and ordered —
Whatever it was — with a soft assurance
That made me mad as I stood behind him,
Gripping his death, and waited. — Coward,
I think, is the name the world has given
To men like me; but I 'll swear I never
Thought of my own disgrace when I shot him . . .
Yes, in the back; — I know it. I know it
Now, but what if I do? . . . As I watched him
Lying there dead in the scattered sawdust,
Wet with a day's blown froth, I noted
That things were still: — that the walnut tables,
Where men but a moment before were sitting,
Were gone; — that a screen of something around
    me
Shut them out of my sight. But the gilded

Signs of a hundred beers and whiskies
Flashed from the walls above, and the mirrors
And glasses behind the bar were lighted
In some strange way, and into my spirit
A thousand shafts of terrible fire
Burned like death, and I fell. — The story
Of what came then, you know.

                                 But tell me,
What does the whole thing mean? — What are
    we —
Slaves of an awful ignorance? — puppets
Pulled by a fiend? — or gods without knowing it?
Do we shut from ourselves our own salvation, —
Or what do we do! — I tell you, Domine,
There are times in the lives of us poor devils
When heaven and hell get mixed: — though con-
    science
May come like a whisper of Christ to warn us
Away from our sins, it is lost or laughed at, —
And then we fall.   And for all who have fallen—
Even for him — I hold no malice,
Nor much compassion: a mightier mercy
Than mine must shrieve him. — And I, — I am
    going
Into the light? — or into the darkness?
Why do I sit through these sickening hours,
And hope? — Good God! are they hours! —
    hours? . . .
Yes! — I am done with days. — And to-morrow —
We two may meet! . . . To-morrow! . . . To-
    morrow! . . .

Afterword

LOOKING back now, a century having passed, one sees and hears very clearly the dreadful sameness of the poetry Robinson encountered in the magazines of his youth, magazines Robinson himself could scarcely get a hearing in. The versification was competently banal, the diction was usually archaic or otherwise stilted, the subject matter was self-consciously poetical. Nor was this the worst that could be said of it. It was much then as it is today: only certain views, only certain feelings were felt to be proper for poetry. (Of course, our acceptable views differ vastly from those of a hundred years ago.) It is no more than a slight exaggeration to claim, with Malcolm Cowley, that all books and magazines intended for the parlor table at the tail-end of the genteel tradition were to be kept as "innocent as milk." It was this piety of sentiment that seems so tiresome now and from which Robinson quite deliberately though politely turned aside. This first book of his had in it, he was to boast, "very little tinkling water," and there was not a single "red-bellied robin" in the whole collection.

Yet superficially Robinson's poems may strike us as being very much of a piece with the generality of American poetry of the nineties. Robinson's techniques were more or less the same as those of his contemporaries, the meters strict always, so strict and even jingly at times as to suggest light verse. Only—and this makes all the difference—the pieties are not quite in place, the pieties that made his more esteemed contemporaries (poets like Gilder and Aldrich and Stedman, names to conjure with at the time) acceptable to the dying literary culture of the day. Pieties there still are in Robinson, and this is surely one of the reasons for the undeniable decline of his reputation, since even Robinson's darker pieties have by now inevitably become those of a vanished past. But there is a fundamental gravity in the demeanor of his verse that gives it character, hidden often behind a characteristic veil of humor. The voice of his poems is that of a somewhat melancholy bachelor uncle, with at times a twinkle in his eye, caused, one may suspect, by a glass of spirits nipped in secret.

The Torrent and The Night Before is the first sign in verse of the stirring of some new thing already felt in certain recent novels and stories. Once Robinson had opened the package of small blue-backed books he had paid $52 to have printed, once he had begun to address the 312 copies to the lucky recipients he had chosen, he was—he had become—the first modern American poet. This debut is less famous than Whitman's, and certainly less revolutionary, but it will do, and what fame it bears is not misplaced. The work in it is surprisingly mature, even the poems that go wrong, as most of them predictably do. Still, four or five small masterpieces are here to be discovered, poems that even before the century turned had become anthology pieces and would remain so ever after, "Luke Havergal" most resoundingly. There is something unutterably fascinating about the beginnings of a writer, however imperfect the first works themselves may be. In them we seem to discern marks of the future, sketchy outlines of all that is to come. So much at least is true of this modest, brave volume.

And what a pleasure it must have been to receive a copy of it in the mails that first December of Robinson's long life as a poet. One of the astonishing things about this little book is that so many readers immediately recognized its powers, though it was to be some twenty years before Robinson's genius was widely acknowledged. Eighteen or more reviews of the book were to reach print—far more than most first books of poetry receive these days—and most were favorable. Strangers to whom he had dispatched hopeful copies, important literary or academic personages, replied with praise. (Thomas Hardy, just then turning to poetry at the close of his career as a novelist, was an exception, failing to acknowledge the copy the young Robinson had sent him; too bad, for the two poets have much in common.) All in all, the response must have been heartening. It cannot have been common in Robinson's day; certainly today it would be exceedingly rare. His faith in himself, never wholly absent even in the darkest days, was now set in place for good. The poems for which he had not, as he said, been able to "foresee oblivion" had escaped their author; they had escaped into the world.

Donald Justice
Iowa City, Iowa
March 26, 1996

Printing Notes

ONLY 312 copies of the 1896 edition of Robinson's first book were produced for him by the Riverside Press of Cambridge, Massachusetts. He received his books in late November, 1896, less than a week after his mother's tragic death. He did not try to sell his book and gave his copies away. His earliest inscriptions date from December, 1896.

There is a significant errata: the first line on page 7 is missing. "They danced and they drank and their souls grew gay," is how the missing line should read. Robinson corrected the line, by hand, in some copies.

Exactly 1,312 copies of this, the Tilbury House edition, were printed in time for the first E.A. Robinson Poetry Festival, held during May, 1996, in Gardiner, Maine. Visiting poets at the festival were Robert Mezey, Rachel Hadas, and Donald Justice.

Proceeds from the sale of this book will benefit the Gardiner Public Library. Special thanks to Library Director Glenna Nowell for her generous assistance in this project. The copy of *The Torrent and The Night Before* used to make this centennial edition was donated to the library by Mr. Edward Sandford Martin. Laura Richards, herself a Pulitzer Prize winner, resident of Gardiner, and friend to Robinson, presented Martin's copy for him in person on December 10, 1936.

Our cover portrait, also from the Gardiner Public Library Collection, shows Robinson as he looked in his high school years, when he first began to write the poems that appear in this book. For the cover of his self-published edition, Robinson chose to print only the book's title in italic display type. The two lines of black-inked letters on blue-green wrappers read, quite simply,

The Torrent &
The Night Before

In 1990, upon our founding, we named our press after the representational name for Gardiner—Tilbury Town—that Robinson used in his poetry. This is the first time we have printed any of his poems.

Mark Melnicove, Publisher